Emotional Healing Trilogy
Book 1

LIES,   LIES,   LIES

Healing Workbook

DR. MICHELLE K-A HAMILTON NMD MDiv

BALBOA.PRESS
A DIVISION OF HAY HOUSE

Balboa Press books may be ordered through booksellers or by contacting:

Balboa Press
A Division of Hay House
1663 Liberty Drive
Bloomington, IN 47403
www.balboapress.com
844-682-1282

Scripture quotations marked KJV are from the Holy Bible, King James Version (Authorized Version). First published in 1611. Quoted from the KJV Classic Reference Bible, Copyright © 1983 by The Zondervan Corporation.

Print information available on the last page.

ISBN: 979-8-7652-4512-5 (sc)
ISBN: 979-8-7652-4511-8 (e)

Library of Congress Control Number: 2023917667

Balboa Press rev. date: 11/06/2023

FOREWORD

These six things doth the Lord Hate:
Yea, seven are an abomination unto to him:
A proud look, a lying tongue,
And hands that shed innocent blood,
An heart that deviseth wicked imaginations,
Feet that be swift in running to mischief,
A false witness that speaketh lies,
And he that soweth discord among brethren.

Proverbs 6:16-19 KJV

-The Holy Spirit

CONTENTS

ACKNOWLEDGMENTS

In the words of Nelson Mandela, "It always seems impossible until it is done." I could not have embarked on this journey alone. I thank God for giving me hope with each new day and for the Holy Spirit's guidance. My family has molded me into who I am today because of love, unity, and forgiveness. I wish to thank my brother Tarick for being a tower of strength when I needed him most—I sincerely thank my adoptive mothers, who stepped in with encouraging words along the way. My friends who support my projects and provide feedback, I am forever indebted to you all for the prayers, calls, and constant encouragement and nudge to write, write, write. I pray that I am a source of motivation for you all as you have been for me. One last thing, please consider this quote below:

"Perhaps, instead of asking questions of our trials, our trials
are meant to ask questions of ourselves."

"One Night with the King Quotes." *Quotes.net.* STANDS4 LLC, 2021.
Web. 5 Feb. 2021. <https://www.quotes.net/mquote/1048724>.

Thank You, Love Always

MKAH

CHAPTER 1

THE FIRST EMOTIONAL TRAUMA

Another busy day; it was now 6 a.m. and time to prep for the store. Annie's morning routine would seem effortless to an observer. Still, it took a lot of planning for Annie to keep organized. It was the early 80's, and Jack had fulfilled Annie's dream of having a family. She just needed to continue pressing forward with her financial and business plans.

Annie's early life had been traumatic, but she had a resilient spirit and yielded to no one. Today would change her life forever. It was a hot summer's day, and Sonia had experienced something strange and wanted to share it with her mom, Annie. As they packed the fridge together, Sonia decided it was time to say something: Mom, I think something is happening with Daddy and Joan. What do you mean? Annie asked. Well, he looks at her the same way he looks at you. Joan was the daughter of Annie's best friend, who needed lodging while attending a training program in the city. Annie's big heart could not say no to her friend as it assisted them greatly. Annie paused, looked at Sonia briefly, and then kept silently working. The next few days were business as usual until it all exploded.

The thoughts kept ruminating in her mind, and she searched Joan's belongings while she was away, hoping to find a clue or perhaps nothing to prove her daughters' suspicion. Unfortunately, she found a note with her husband's initials and recognized the handwriting.

Annie's heart sank, her thoughts rushing. She tucked it back, dressed, and left the house hurriedly. It was early afternoon when she arrived at Joan's training center. Annie asked the security for Joan Harris, and he directed her to the cafeteria where the trainees had been gathered for a seminar. As Annie made her way to the cafe, tears filled her eyes, and she started to sweat even more. She asked an instructor to call Joan at the door and back of the cafeteria as she had an urgent message. The instructor moved toward the seated students and asked Joan

Harris to come to the back of the cafeteria. Joan went to the back in a few minutes, and they both stepped outside the building.

With a raging rush, Annie grabbed Joan by the collar, shaking Joan and shouting, "How could you do this?" How could you? Joan started to cry as Annie's rage escalated, and she slapped her across the face several times. Humiliated by her conduct, Joan spoke not a word. By this time, a few persons heard the shouting and stopped to look. Annie regained her composure and left for home. She felt defeated, abused, and betrayed as she went home, and her anger increased again.

Annie had never verbally or physically behaved in such a manner before. Annie's thoughts mingled with fear and anger, and she wanted out of her marriage.

Where did it begin? Why do people choose to lie? One author states that it has a father who created it, and humans inherit it genetically from their forefathers. Lies are deeply rooted in the acts and consequences of sin based on theology. However, our society dictates that some people lie because of their astrological or zodiac signs at birth. For every action, there is a reaction deemed positive or negative. Therefore, it is the act of choosing to lie that will ultimately lead to undetermined consequences.

The very nature of a lie involves a deep emotional desire for self, which can never lead to true happiness. It is as if a story is born with each lie, and the plot thickens as it becomes an unending story with twists and turns. Most often, the progenitor of the lie does not realize the holes in the plot until later, forcing the creation of another cover-up to the original falsified event.

Creativity has its' place, and it is remarkable how someone's entire life can revolve around a lie. Lies can destroy an entire family, and pain can last a lifetime and influence the path and choices of each individual in the family. Review the biblical examples of lies as told in the bible in the stories below:

Nehemiah 6:1-9 – Sanballat's plot to hinder Nehemiah

1 Now it came to pass, when Sanballat, and Tobiah, and Geshem the Arabian, and the rest of our enemies, heard that I had built the wall, and that there was no breach left therein; (though at that time I had not set up the doors upon the gates;) 2 That Sanballat and Geshem sent unto me, saying, Come, let us meet together in some one of the villages in the plain of Ono. But they thought to do me mischief. 3 And I sent messengers unto them, saying, I am doing a

great work, so that I cannot come down: why should the work cease, whilst I leave it, and come down to you? 4 Yet they sent unto me four times after this sort; and I answered them after the same manner. 5 Then sent Sanballat his servant unto me in like manner the fifth time with an open letter in his hand; 6 Wherein was written, It is reported among the heathen, and Gashmu saith it, that thou and the Jews think to rebel: for which cause thou buildest the wall, that thou mayest be their king, according to these words. 7 And thou hast also appointed prophets to preach of thee at Jerusalem, saying, There is a king in Judah: and now shall it be reported to the king according to these words. Come now therefore, and let us take counsel together. 8 Then I sent unto him, saying, There are no such things done as thou sayest, but thou feignest them out of thine own heart. 9 For they all made us afraid, saying, Their hands shall be weakened from the work, that it be not done. Now therefore, O God, strengthen my hands.

Acts 5:1-11 – The death of Ananias and Sapphira

1 But a certain man named Ananias, with Sapphira his wife, sold a possession, 2 And kept back part of the price, his wife also being privy to it, and brought a certain part, and laid it at the apostles' feet. 3 But Peter said, Ananias, why hath Satan filled thine heart to lie to the Holy Ghost, and to keep back part of the price of the land? 4 Whiles it remained, was it not thine own? and after it was sold, was it not in thine own power? why hast thou conceived this thing in thine heart? thou hast not lied unto men, but unto God. 5 And Ananias hearing these words fell down, and gave up the ghost: and great fear came on all them that heard these things. 6 And the young men arose, wound him up, and carried him out, and buried him. 7 And it was bout the space of three hours after, when his wife, not knowing what was done, came in. 8 And Peter answered unto her, Tell me whether ye sold the land for so much? And she said, Yea, for so much. 9 Then Peter said unto her, How is it that ye have agreed together to tempt the Spirit of the Lord? behold, the feet of them which have buried thy husband are at the door, and shall carry thee out. 10 Then fell she down straightway at his feet, and yielded up the ghost: and the young men came in, and found her dead, and, carrying her forth, buried her by her husband. 11 And great fear came upon all the church, and upon as many as heard these things.

1Samuel 27:8-12 - David deceives Achish

8 And David and his men went up, and invaded the Geshurites, and the Gezrites, and the Amalekites: for those nations were of old the inhabitants of the land, as thou goest to Shur, even unto the land of Egypt. 9 And David smote the land, and left neither man nor woman alive, and took away the sheep, and the oxen, and the asses, and the camels, and the apparel, and

returned, and came to Achish. 10 And Achish said, Whither have ye made a road to day? And David said, Against the south of Judah, and against the south of the Jerahmeelites, and against the south of the Kenites. 11 And David saved neither man nor woman alive, to bring tidings to Gath, saying, Lest they should tell on us, saying, So did David, and so will be his manner all the while he dwelleth in the country of the Philistines. 12 And Achish believed David, saying, He hath made his people Israel utterly to abhor him; therefore he shall be my servant for ever.

Jeremiah 40:7-16 - A conspiracy against Gedaliah

7 Now when all the captains of the forces which were in the fields, even they and their men, heard that the king of Babylon had made Gedaliah the son of Ahikam governor in the land, and had committed unto him men, and women, and children, and of the poor of the land, of them that were not carried away captive to Babylon; 8 Then they came to Gedaliah to Mizpah, even Ishmael the son of Nethaniah, and Johanan and Jonathan the sons of Kareah, and Seraiah the son of Tanhumeth, and the sons of Ephai the Netophathite, and Jezaniah the son of a Maachathite, they and their men. 9 And Gedaliah the son of Ahikam the son of Shaphan sware unto them and to their men, saying, Fear not to serve the Chaldeans: dwell in the land, and serve the king of Babylon, and it shall be well with you. 10 As for me, behold, I will dwell at Mizpah to serve the Chaldeans, which will come unto us: but ye, gather ye wine, and summer fruits, and oil, and put them in your vessels, and dwell in your cities that ye have taken. 11 Likewise when all the Jews that were in Moab, and among the Ammonites, and in Edom, and that were in all the countries, heard that the king of Babylon had left a remnant of Judah, and that he had set over them Gedaliah the son of Ahikam the son of Shaphan; 12 Even all the Jews returned out of all places whither they were driven, and came to the land of Judah, to Gedaliah, unto Mizpah, and gathered wine and summer fruits very much. 13 Moreover Johanan the son of Kareah, and all the captains of the forces that were in the fields, came to Gedaliah to Mizpah, 14 And said unto him, Dost thou certainly know that Baalis the king of the Ammonites hath sent Ishmael the son of Nethaniah to slay thee? But Gedaliah the son of Ahikam believed them not. 15 Then Johanan the son of Kareah spake to Gedaliah in Mizpah secretly, saying, Let me go, I pray thee, and I will slay Ishmael the son of Nethaniah, and no man shall know it: wherefore should he slay thee, that all the Jews which are gathered unto thee should be scattered, and the remnant in Judah perish? 16 But Gedaliah the son of Ahikam said unto Johanan the son of Kareah, Thou shalt not do this thing: for thou speakest falsely of Ishmael.

CHAPTER 2

LIFE CHANGES

The relationship between Annie and her friend Cynthia, Joan's mom, would no longer be the same. Shame and guilt separated the two friends. Although each grieved for the other's loss and emotional trauma, the shame of the event had a profound, almost palpable effect. Each member questioned trust, integrity, and love; betrayal was a constant emotional climate that manifested physically in Annie's persona—shattering the family she had built. It seemed that her past had become her future again. The unhappiness she experienced during her early years in a broken family caused by betrayal was recycled, and she could not escape it.

Annie's wound got more profound in the passing days, and she could not see herself living with Jack and being able to trust him again. She searched her memories, analyzing them for encounters with friends, looking for links to determine if this was indeed the first act of infidelity. As she visualized every meeting possible of interactions with women over the years, it appeared every small gesture was a possible type of flirting that she overlooked. Her anger raged, and she felt naive, and he never loved her. Every memory of their courtship started to seem like an act in which she was a victim of what, at the time, she considered his "charm" but now looked like manipulation.

It was time to move on, but how? Annie wanted to move on without Jack, but his male presence in the home gave a sense of security. Fear of losing a male presence made her feel vulnerable. As the months went by, this segregated her once-happy family. The children spoke only in her presence, and Jack silently moved in and around the home in silence as his presence became less evident to all. Only conversations of necessity were present from day to day.

The atmosphere of the home grew cold and silent. It became more apparent to Annie that something had to change as it felt like a thick fog, and everyone in the house appeared to be at risk of suffocating in unhappiness. As she prayed about the situation, her main concern was safety. Her prayers morphed into a pleading for God's guidance, coverage, and protection if she told Jack she wanted a divorce.

The day finally came as Annie was overwhelmed in tears after having dinner on her patio. She felt the burden lifted as she felt God's assurance that he was ultimately protecting her. She need not fear for the future with or without Jack. The penultimate conversation occurred mid-week when Jack came home late one night. Annie told Jack she wanted a divorce and that he needed to move out of the home by the end of the month. Jack's response was predictable as he spoke about the likely vulnerability to thieves as he would no longer be present, and it was because of his presence they had been safe over the years. Annie told Jack she would trust God to care for her. She admitted that once she was fearful, she no longer would allow her fears to keep her joined to an unfaithful spouse and an unhappy home.

During the months prior Jack did not deny his infidelity and Joan confessed what had happened. In her time of need she felt confused with Jack's gestures and believed if she did not comply the room and board would no longer be available and this would result in her dropping out the training program because her mom could not afford to pay for private room and boarding.

Jack took advantage of her situation to satisfy his own adulterous tendencies and plunged his family in pain, ruin and defeat. Why would a man seek to do such a selfish act? Is there a connection to his own upbringing that could have influenced this path or is there a link to the exposure in the society or relationship experience that could influence such a behavior? There are many sides to a story and truth often times is the hardest to find. The action of mankind to deviate from the path of truth mixed with lies results in poor choices.

CHAPTER 3

THE ANATOMY AND PHYSIOLOGY OF LIES (STRUCTURE AND FUNCTION)

The book of Hebrews, chapter 6, verse 18, denotes God's immutability and impossible ability to lie. Balaam, his servant in Numbers chapter 23 verse 19, reminded Balak, "God is not a man that he should lie." From these two accounts, we can deduce that the origin of lies begins with God's created beings. The very definition of the word lie in the English language has two varied meanings. As an intransitive verb denoting "position" or an "act of deception" by someone.

In medicine, we study the human body under the branch of biology called 'Anatomy and Physiology, which is the structure and function of the human body. Suppose we superimpose Anatomy and Physiology over the word 'LIE' in the context of the definition presenting false or misleading statements. In that case, this is what we may see:

Structure (Anatomy) – thoughts, motive, and action

Function (Physiology) – Consequences

The structure of a lie is formed in the mind by our very thoughts, which are born by our motives. An individual does not automatically tell a lie, but its' same root comes from a desire.

What is this desire? Let's return to the origin or 1st lie we recorded in history. It appears in Genesis chapter 3, verses 1 through 8. Here, we have recorded an act of deception. As the serpent approached Eve, this was not by chance but by design. The fall of Lucifer marks the very root of this event. Ezekiel chapter 28, verses 11 through 17, points us to the first act of iniquity or sin.

In studying these verses, we see Lucifer, God's perfect creation whose heart was lifted because of beauty and thus coveting his Creator – GOD. The results lead to Lucifer's thoughts and motives desiring to be like the Creator of the universe. Here, "LIES" the structure and function/anatomy and physiology of the first lie.

As the story unfolds, Lucifer, now with intent, persuades the other heavenly beings with his selfish desires by impressing on their minds the desire for more, which results in the continuous genetic snip and posterity of lies. We can now review Genesis chapter 3, verses 1 through 6, where we directly connect the serpents, eliciting the thought that something was missing. The serpent's voice implied that there were more desirable benefits as it spoke to Eve in the garden. It is our freedom of choice that allows us to have the ability to consider new ideas. If we did not have this ability, God's very character and immutability would be a lie!

As such, Eve exercised free will, and we see the birth of neuronal connections fed by the desire to know more. Our brains tend to form new neural pathways based on our thoughts, which can influence our innate desires. The serpent offered Eve something more. Unbeknownst to Eve, she birthed a motive that guided her thought process to the final action. As we know through religious studies, this action resulted in many consequences. The earthly genetic snip was not present, and the foundation laid for the probability of a consistent cycle given the suitable climate in the heart of humanity.

Our structure is constant in human anatomy, but mankind's physiology or function can be altered consistently. The structure of lies is consistent, but humans can change the lying process because of freedom of choice. Thus, the key is 'CHOICE'. The option is given to all and is a powerful tool that requires much contemplation as it can determine our eternal destiny. When one decides to lie, each act or occasion creates and sets up a pathway in our thoughts for continuous growth and reproduction. Let us now identify the limitations of a lie. If we can reproduce lies through our thoughts and motives, we can control their growth and, ultimately, rebirth in our own lives.

READ THE LAST PARAGRAPH AGAIN!

CHAPTER 4

THE HEALTH CONNECTION

Annie's decision towards Jack was to end the marriage. Annie experienced mixed feelings of anger, anxiety, and fear. She felt betrayed, and her ability and desire to trust anyone for the next ten years was null and void. After their separation, Annie resolved to focus on her career and to become successful, thus defying the odds and not allowing a failed marriage to define or hinder her future goals.

As fragile people, we all can search within ourselves for purpose and courage in adversity. As we face life's turns, in the most traumatic moments, we can make a more profound connection spiritually. At this moment, we can also choose how or if we want to overcome our challenges. Many of us prefer to chart a course based on the trauma and chain ourselves to the past, thus allowing it to guide our choices for the future out of pain and fear. Many of us also choose to accept the past, leave it behind, and make the resolution not to allow a traumatic event to plot the path for the future but to look deeper for its true purpose and plot a course to the best version of ourselves. People who do not allow the past to define their future will not let fear or pain guide them but allow themselves to receive forgiveness and hope.

While it was hard over the next few years, Annie had to work on her anger that would surface involuntarily by any triggers of her failed marriage. It could be a friend asking if she keeps in touch with Jack after seeing an object or recalling an event that triggered a memory of Jack and the times they spent together. Annie questioned if he was ever sincere during their marriage during these triggers. She felt betrayed and thought to herself she was not enough for him. Annie was chained to her past but did not know it.

Over time, Annie became anxious and fearful of males who would try to date her over the years. She thought her success in business as a single woman and mother made her vulnerable to men who always told her she needed a male figure to protect her. Nevertheless, Annie developed a habit of praying whenever feeling overwhelmed, and, over the years, as a result, Annie was not easily swayed. Praying provided hope and a sense of assurance she had not felt before.

Many individuals often ignore their emotions and the physiological impact on the body. Psychoneurphysiology is a new frontier in health. Our brain controls several body systems and specific areas control and is affected by our emotions. These include the following:

❖ Breathing Centers of the Brain

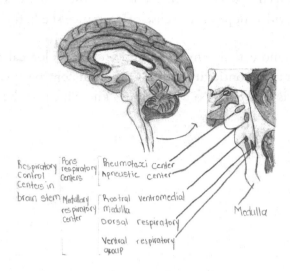

Respiratory Control Centers in brain stem

Pons respiratory Centers
- Pneumotaxi Center
- Apneustic Center

Medullary respiratory Center
- Rostral Ventromedial medulla
- Dorsal respiratory
- Ventral respiratory group

Medulla

Breathing and Emotions

1. Breathing rate increases when you are afraid or anxious. This can lead to hyperventilation, which will cause less oxygen to your brain.
2. Hyperventilation can cause dizziness, elevated heart rate, high blood pressure, blurred vision, and tingling sensations.
3. Breathing slowly can reduce blood pressure and improve the digestion of food and nutrients absorbed from each meal.

❖ The Brain and Motor function

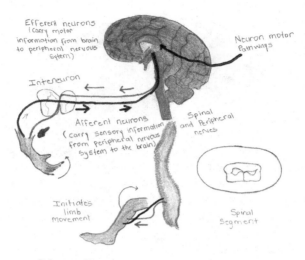

Efferent neurons (carry motor information from brain to peripheral nervous system)

Neuron motor pathways

Interneuron

Afferent neurons (carry sensory information from peripheral nervous system to the brain)

Spinal and Peripheral nerves

Initiates limb movement

Spinal Segment

Motor Function and Emotions

Emotions are a part of the mind-body connection. Think about the last time you felt really happy. Did you feel more energetic light on your feet and could not stop smiling? Perhaps you are feeling sad and noticing you felt tired, had back or joint pains, and even noticed your body movements slowing down? Emotions trigger several body systems, and the brain sends messages to these organs, including the limbs (hands and feet).

❖ Amygdala

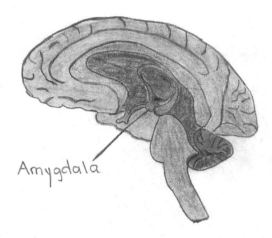

Amygdala

The amygdala's volume increases with exposure to early life stressors and chronic stress. The amygdala controls fear and anxiety. Our relationships and experiences can influence the size of our amygdala. If your relationships has caused you much fear or anxiety the volume of your amygdala which results in a trigger response. This occurs when you find yourself becoming anxious or feeling fearful very easily and may include digestive issues such as bloating, indigestion, acid reflux, anxiety attacks, trust issues, constipation and even hypertension.

❖ Hippocampus

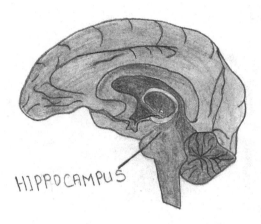

HIPPOCAMPUS

The hippocampus shrinks under early life stress and chronic stress. The hippocampus is responsible for our emotions, memory, and imagination. This can manifest in conditions such as: depression, procrastinating, apathy and so much more.

❖ Pre-frontal cortex

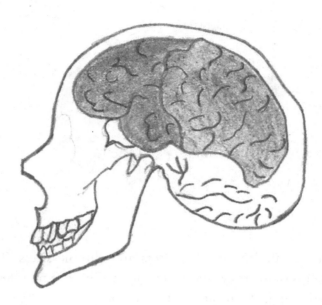

1. The Pre-frontal cortex is responsible for personality, decision-making, and behavior.
2. Emotional regulation and well-being strongly affect our amygdala and pre-frontal cortex.
3. Chronic stress or exposure to early life stressors can decrease sections of the pre-frontal cortex.

Examples of Personality and Behavioral Disorders

Personality Disorders	Behavioral Disorders
1. Narcissistic Personality	1. Attention-deficit hyperactivity disorder (ADHD)
2. Dependent Personality disorder	
3. Avoidant Personality disorder	2. Oppositional defiant disorder (ODD)
4. Borderline Personality disorder	3. Conduct disorder
5. Paranoid Personality	4. Intermittent explosive disorder (IED)
6. Antisocial personality disorder (ASPD)	5. Disruptive mood dysregulation disorder (DMDD)

For each part of the brain in the previous pictures, we now connect Annie's recall of negative experiences and the emotions triggered, which included fear, anger, and anxiety, and see the parts of the brain affected and, to some extent, the effect on the brain and the rest of the body. Consider the pathway that multiple triggers affect and consider the repetition over time. Just think about it! Annie had years of recall of Jack's betrayal of her trust and the lies that spiraled to cover this unfaithfulness. Reenacting scenes as a result of broken dreams leads to bitter memories.

We cannot separate our emotions from our physical health. During intense anger, our digestive system (stomach) becomes impaired as fewer digestive enzymes are present, leading to indigestion, bloating, gas, constipation, and GERD (acid reflux). The same can happen with the experience of anxiety and fear. Over several years, this recurring process leads to ill health that eventually manifests in improper nutrition and even diabetes.

The lack of a sound digestive system with symptoms of bloating, gas, and GERD (acid reflux) eventually leads to food elimination to prevent recurrence or control symptoms. These food restrictions for many people include healthy, nutritious foods. Therefore, this ultimately contributes to nutritional deficiencies in the future.

Lie, Lies, Lies, its very structure and function also affect the human system and processes. For those whose lives catastrophic lies have impacted, you may be able to relate. For those accused of these lies, I hope you can glimpse its devastating effects.

There are many sides to a story, and a common saying is that a story has three sides. They are my side, your side, and the truth! The truth may consist of some elements of both sides of the story plus the actual event or circumstances. We cannot justify a wrongful act, but we can learn to look at each other views to find a resolution to a problem and move forward. As such, let us now transition into moving forward as I ask you, the reader, to write the next chapter of this book.

CHAPTER 5

MY CHAPTER - WORKSHEET 1 – MY EXPERIENCE

1. Lies Told To Me

_____
_____
_____
_____
_____
_____
_____
_____
_____
_____
_____
_____
_____
_____
_____
_____
_____
_____
_____

2. How have these lies impacted my life?

_____

_____

_____

_____

_____

_____

_____

_____

_____

_____

_____

_____

_____

_____

_____

_____

_____

_____

_____

_____

_____

_____

_____

_____

_____

_____

_____

_____

_____

3. Lies I have told

_____

_____

_____

_____

_____

_____

_____

_____

_____

_____

_____

_____

_____

_____

_____

_____

_____

_____

_____

_____

_____

_____

_____

_____

_____

_____

_____

_____

_____

_____

_____

_____

4. How have the lies I have told impacted my life and other individuals?

_____
_____
_____
_____
_____
_____
_____
_____
_____
_____
_____
_____
_____
_____
_____
_____
_____
_____
_____
_____
_____
_____
_____
_____
_____
_____
_____
_____
_____

Worksheet 2 - Healing the Past

Everyone needs forgiveness. Forgiveness is not forgetting the past, as this is impossible. Still, it is a process of reviewing the past hurt or experience and, through a bigger lens, learning to reframe your story, which considers both sides, leading to empathy and, thus, forgiveness.

Forgiveness is not for the offender. It is for you, and it does not mean you will forget the act or are excusing the incident. It may not always lead to reconciliation, but it will lead to recovering your peace and provide a path for navigating the future.

According to Dr. Dick Tibbits, forgiveness begins when you can work through these ten principles:

THE TEN PRINCIPLES OF FORGIVENESS

1. **Accept** that life is unfair and that others may play by a different set of rules than you do.
   - o   I accept life is not fair [ ] Yes [ ] No

2. **Stop** blaming others for your circumstances.
   - o   I do not blame others [ ]
   - o   I am praying about not blaming others [ ]

3. **Understand** that you cannot change the person who hurt you; you can only change yourself.
   - o   I can only change myself [ ]
   - o   I am willing to allow God to help me to change [ ]

4. **Acknowledge** the anger and hurt that some unpleasant or even harmful event is causing you.
   - o   I still experience anger or hurt from past experiences [ ] YES [ ] NO

5. **Reframe** your "grievance story" by placing the hurtful events in a broader context than your current point of view.
   - o   I am willing to review my story to see the bigger picture from both sides [ ] YES [ ] NO

6. **Recognize** that only you can choose to forgive.
   - o   I am choosing to forgive today [ ] YES [ ] NO

7. **Shift** your view of the offender by humbly empathizing with their life situation.
   o   I am now able to empathize with those who offend me [ ] YES [ ] NO

8. **Move** intentionally from discontent toward contentment.
   o   I am ready to experience contentment [ ] YES [ ] NO

9. **Understand** that forgiveness will take time and cannot be rushed.
   o   I need more time to forgive [ ] YES [ ] NO
   o   I am ready to forgive today [ ] YES

10. **Take** responsibility for your life and your future
    o   Today, I take responsibility for my future and move from the past [ ] YES [ ] NO

CHAPTER 6

TO THINE OWN SELF BE
TRUE FOR POSTERITY

Although we are not at ACT 1 Scene III of Hamlet, the phrase "To thine own self be true" remains relevant today. We can use the phrase in the context of being honest and committed to play our part in building healthy relationships.

Who we are when no one is watching can be eye-opening, so what about taking that time to contemplate what your words transcend for the future? Suppose you can accept that we all have equal opportunity to choose, be honest, and desire to be persons of integrity. In that case, we collectively poise ourselves to influence the future and the lives of those we interact with daily.

Maya Angelou says it best as she wrote, "I've learned that people will forget what you said, people will forget what you did, but people will never forget how you made them feel."

Choose today to bring joy, peace, harmony, love, respect, and forgiveness to find peace in the present and hope for the future.

Annie's pain healed when she was able to forgive Jack. They had a healthy friendship when she could reframe her story of his indiscretions despite not knowing if he continued on the same trajectory in other relationships. She could live again and build a new relationship with God and her life partner.

The CHOICE is yours; what will your 1st step be:

1. Asking God for forgiveness?
2. Forgiving someone who has wronged you?
3. Pray and ask God to give you a heart of forgiveness.

We all make choices daily, and to this end, they vary from conscious or unconscious decisions. Make your choice count today for the future.

- ❖ C –claiming
- ❖ H-healing
- ❖ O-overcoming
- ❖ I - inner
- ❖ C–conflict
- ❖ E-eternally

CHAPTER 7

WHAT'S MY EQ? (EMOTIONAL QUOTIENT SCORE)

One last thing: are you able to recognize your own emotions as well as others? Can you discern the difference between different feelings and label them? Let's test your emotional ability by taking the Emotional Intelligence Analysis on the next few pages.

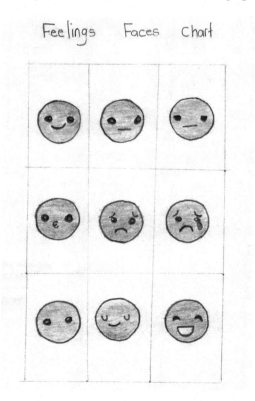

Feelings Faces Chart

My Emotional Intelligence Analysis

What is Emotional Intelligence? According to the Cambridge Dictionary, it is "The ability to understand and control your feelings, and to understand the feelings of others and appropriately react to them."

Take this EQ quiz to know how well you can identify your feelings and those of others. It will help to guide your thinking, behavior, and response to adapt or adjust your emotions.

This quiz will enable you to identify these five components:

1. Self-awareness
2. Self-regulation
3. Motivation
4. Empathy
5. Social skills

Instructions:

Step 1. ***Assess and score*** each of the questionnaire's statements.

Score your assessment using a scale where

- **1** indicates that the statement ***does NOT apply at all***
- **3** indicates that the statement ***applies about half the time***
- **5** indicates that the statement ***ALWAYS applies to you***

Step 2 & 3 ***Total and interpret your results***

- Transfer your scores to the calculation table and total your results.

#	How much does each statement apply to you	Mark your score				
	Read each statement and decide how strongly the information applies to YOU. Score yourself 1 to 5 based on the following guide. 1 = Does not apply ~ 3 = Applies half the time ~ 5 = Always applies	Choose the number that shows how strongly the statement applies				
		A	B	C	D	E
1	I can realize as soon as I lose my temper	1	2	3	4	5
2	I can 'reframe' bad situations quickly	1	2	3	4	5
3	I can always motivate myself to do difficult tasks	1	2	3	4	5
4	I am always able to see things from the other person's viewpoint	1	2	3	4	5
5	I am an excellent listener	1	2	3	4	5
6	I know when I am happy	1	2	3	4	5
7	I do not wear my 'heart on my sleeve	1	2	3	4	5
8	I am usually able to prioritize important activities at work and get on with them	1	2	3	4	5
9	I am excellent at empathizing with someone else's problem	1	2	3	4	5
10	I never interrupt other people's conversations	1	2	3	4	5
11	I usually recognize when I am stressed	1	2	3	4	5
12	Others can rarely tell what kind of mood I am in	1	2	3	4	5
13	I always meet deadlines	1	2	3	4	5
14	I can tell if someone is not happy with me	1	2	3	4	5
15	I am good at adapting and mixing with a variety of people	1	2	3	4	5
16	When I am being 'emotional,' I am aware of this	1	2	3	4	5
17	I rarely 'fly off the handle' at other people	1	2	3	4	5

#	How much does each statement apply to you	Mark your score				
	Read each statement and decide how strongly the information applies to YOU. Score yourself 1 to 5 based on the following guide. 1 = Does not apply ~ 3 = Applies half the time ~ 5 = Always applies	Choose the number that shows how strongly the statement applies				
		A	B	C	D	E
18	I never waste time	1	2	3	4	5
19	I can tell if a team of people is not getting along with each other	1	2	3	4	5
20	People are the most interesting thing in life for me	1	2	3	4	5
21	When I feel anxious, I usually can account for the reason(s)	1	2	3	4	5
22	Difficult people do not annoy me	1	2	3	4	5
23	I do not prevaricate (tell untruth)	1	2	3	4	5
24	I can usually understand why people are being difficult towards me	1	2	3	4	5
25	I love to meet new people and get to know what makes them 'tick.'	1	2	3	4	5
26	I always know when I'm being unreasonable	1	2	3	4	5
27	I can consciously alter my frame of mind or mood	1	2	3	4	5
28	I believe you should do the difficult things first	1	2	3	4	5
29	Other individuals are not 'difficult,' just 'different.'	1	2	3	4	5
30	I need a variety of work colleagues to make my job interesting	1	2	3	4	5
31	Awareness of my own emotions is critical to me at all times	1	2	3	4	5
32	I do not let stressful situations or people affect me once I have left work	1	2	3	4	5
33	Delayed gratification is a virtue that I hold to	1	2	3	4	5
34	I can understand if I am being unreasonable	1	2	3	4	5

#	How much does each statement apply to you	Mark your score				
	Read each statement and decide how strongly the information applies to YOU. Score yourself 1 to 5 based on the following guide. 1 = Does not apply ~ 3 = Applies half the time ~ 5 = Always applies	Choose the number that shows how strongly the statement applies				
		A	B	C	D	E
35	I like to ask questions to find out what is important to people	1	2	3	4	5
36	I can tell if someone has upset or annoyed me	1	2	3	4	5
37	I rarely worry about work or life in general	1	2	3	4	5
38	I believe in 'Action this Day	1	2	3	4	5
39	I can understand why my actions sometimes offend others	1	2	3	4	5
40	I see working with difficult people as simply a challenge to win them over	1	2	3	4	5
41	I can let anger 'go' quickly so that it no longer affects me	1	2	3	4	5
42	I can suppress my emotions when I need to	1	2	3	4	5
43	I can always motivate myself even when I feel low	1	2	3	4	5
44	I can sometimes see things from others' points of view	1	2	3	4	5
45	I am good at reconciling differences with other people	1	2	3	4	5
46	I know what makes me happy	1	2	3	4	5
47	Others often do not know how I am feeling about things	1	2	3	4	5
48	Motivations have been the key to my success	1	2	3	4	5
49	Reasons for disagreements are always clear to me	1	2	3	4	5
50	I generally build solid relationships with those I work with	1	2	3	4	5

STEP 2

Total and interpret your results

Record your 1, 2, 3, 4, and 5 scores for the questionnaire statements in the grid below. The grid organizes the statements into emotional competency lists.

(A) Self-awareness		(B) Managing emotions		(C) Motivating oneself		(D) Empathy		(E) Social Skill	
1		2		3		4		5	
6		7		8		9		10	
11		12		13		14		15	
16		17		18		19		20	
21		22		23		24		25	
26		27		28		29		30	
31		32		33		34		35	
36		37		38		39		40	
41		42		43		44		45	
46		47		48		49		50	

1. *Calculate* a total for each of the five emotional competencies.

Total = (SA)		Total = (ME)		Total = (MO)		Total = (E)		Total = (SS)	

STEP 3

Interpret your totals for each area of competency using the following guide.

35-50	This area is a ***strength*** for you.
18-34	***Giving attention*** to where you feel you are weakest will pay dividends.
10-17	Make this area a ***development priority***.

STEP 4

Record your result for each emotional competency: strength needs attention or development priority.

	Strength 35-50	Needs attention 18-34	Development priority 10-17
Self-awareness (A)			
Managing emotions (B)			
Motivating oneself (C)			
Empathy (D)			
Social Skill (E)			

It is essential to be able to identify, understand, and manage our emotions in positive ways as it affects our health. Additional benefits include improving communication, empathizing with others, overcoming challenges, and diffusing conflicts.

Areas to improve: *Consider your results and identify one or two actions you can take immediately to strengthen* your *emotional intelligence*.

REFERENCES

Goleman, D. 1995. *Why it can matter more than IQ.* New York: Bantam Books.

Tibbits, Dr. Dick. 2008. *Forgive To Live: How Forgiveness Can Change Your Life.* Thomas Nelson Publishers.

The Bible: King James Version

Photos/Drawings

Artist – Andrew Chin
- Faces

Artist – Grace-Ann Brown
- Breathing Centers of the Brain
- Motor Function and the Brain
- The Amygdala
- The Hippocampus:
- The Pre-frontal Cortex
- Emotions Chart
- Road Directions

ABOUT THE AUTHOR

Dr. Michelle Hamilton BSc, M.Div., NMD
Naturopathic Physician and Medical Minister

Dr. Michelle Hamilton is a health and business enthusiast with over 20 years of combined business, health care, and global health education experience. Dr. Hamilton holds a B.Sc. in Alternative Medicine from Everglades University in Boca Raton, Florida, a Master's in Divinity from Liberty University, Virginia, and her Medical Doctoral degree from Bastyr University, California, specializing in Naturopathic Medicine.

Over the years, Dr. Hamilton has been able to combine her educational achievements and experience to address the spiritual, physical, and psychological needs of others. She is known for her compassion, patience, servant leadership, and mentoring within communities and several professional organizations.

Dr. Hamilton has organized community health programs for wellness and conducted workshops in the USA and the Caribbean on natural medicine, spiritual growth, and "Forgiveness for Healthy Living." In addition, she has also conducted monthly seminars for those incarcerated in US correctional facilities as a contribution to the rehabilitation and re-entry program of the states' facility. She owns and operates Hope Centre for Natural Health (USA) and Hope Lifestyle Centers Ltd. (JA), which offers Telemedicine consultation in alternative medicine globally. Dr. Hamilton believes it's essential to empower individuals to take charge of their health and has several programs geared toward health education on various national and online platforms:

NCU TV, NCU Radio – NCU Radio Wellness Week, Its' All Connected, Lifestyle Check, and Hope42Day.

More Hope Today TV (YouTube) – Let's Pray for Your Health and Hope42Day

TVJ - It's All Connected Weekly Health Show

Podbean and Google (Podcast apps) - 3RIVE Weekly

Instagram: I4Give2

Instagram: hope4.2day

MORE HOPE TODAY tv

NOTES

Printed in the United States
by Baker & Taylor Publisher Services